Joseph Kolemou

My dream for the African Union

Joseph Kolemou

My dream for the African Union

ScienciaScripts

Imprint

Any brand names and product names mentioned in this book are subject to trademark, brand or patent protection and are trademarks or registered trademarks of their respective holders. The use of brand names, product names, common names, trade names, product descriptions etc. even without a particular marking in this work is in no way to be construed to mean that such names may be regarded as unrestricted in respect of trademark and brand protection legislation and could thus be used by anyone.

Cover image: www.ingimage.com

This book is a translation from the original published under ISBN 978-620-2-27486-9.

Publisher:
Sciencia Scripts
is a trademark of
Dodo Books Indian Ocean Ltd. and OmniScriptum S.R.L publishing group

120 High Road, East Finchley, London, N2 9ED, United Kingdom
Str. Armeneasca 28/1, office 1, Chisinau MD-2012, Republic of Moldova, Europe
Printed at: see last page
ISBN: 978-620-5-81715-5

Table of contents

I. THE DREAM..3
II. MOBILIZATION TO BRING THE DREAM TO MANY 7
III. THE REALIZATION OF THE DREAM 24

Our respectable African cultures are bridges of rapprochement between peoples and allow us to achieve together the erection of the African Union.

I pay tribute:

-       To my late father and mother: Papa Raphaël and Mama Elisabeth Konomou who gave me life and educated me.

-       To Father Bernard Bouchet, my Professor of Philosophy at the Saint Augustine Major Seminary, located in Samaya, in the Republic of Mali, who gave me the love of wisdom.

-       In memory of the late El hadj Boubacar Soto Diallo, Magistrate, who directed my steps towards the profession of Lawyer.

-       To Maître Boubacar Sow, Lawyer, who contributed to my professional and human training.

I would like to express my gratitude and sincere thanks to them.

I. THE DREAM

The idea of the greatness of a united Africa! Sitting in a chair under the shade of a tree, at sunrise, with his head resting on the palm of his right hand, he never stopped thinking about the greatness of this Africa. This idea haunted him, it was the object of his many meditations and he saw in it the salvation of Africa.

That day, Jo didn't go anywhere. Everyone in his family had gone out to attend to their bureaucratic, scholastic and trade training activities. There was silence around him. He could only hear the songs of birds, the beating of the wings of birds, flies, butterflies and crickets, the meowing of his cat, the growling of his dog, the echoes of distant voices, the blowing of the wind and the sounds that came from the swaying of the foliage, the cracking of dead leaves under the effect of the sun's rays, the noises that came from time to time from the footsteps of those who were passing by and from the rolling machines. A listening of a silence without silence. In this way, there can be no absolute silence in this life. This environment was conducive to his reflection.

This scholar believes that even in traditional Africa, the idea of greatness was crystallized in the hearts of Africans who built great ensembles of living together. Didn't he learn that following the Empire of Ghana, Soundiata Kéita defeated Soumaoro Kanté and extended his Empire over an even larger area? Also in the colonial era, did not certain men, such as El Hadj Oumar Tall, Samory Touré and others, think of building vast ensembles as a strategic means to defeat the colonizing powers?

But in his thought, he conceives that the true greatness resides in the values that we carry and that are expressed in our words and behaviors, in our works, as well as in our links with the transcendent, with the other humans and creatures of the world. Immaterial values that define our identity. They are the pillars that support the construction, which determine the architectural type, the type of man or humanism. He believes that by going down into the bowels of our African earth, into the depths of the African people, we will find the essential stone on which Africa will be built. This work of exploration with discernment and recovery sheds light on who we are and what our vision of life is. Is it not known and testified that the African gives pre-eminence to the group, to the community, to the society in which each individual is nevertheless respected? Values such as solidarity, mutual aid, respect due to the elders, to the elderly and to life, hospitality, belief in God, harmony, respect for one's commitments, courage, work, generosity, dignity, tolerance,... have enabled him to overcome adversity and to make living together possible. For him, the knowledge of the said values in us, the existence of negroid affinities, the historical past, the geographical positions, certain requirements or necessities favor the construction of this vast group that is the African Union. An ambition that is well and truly within the reach of Africans. But in order to achieve this, we need to know where we are now. What were the policies adopted by our African States to achieve the said ambition? A preliminary questioning before any other proposal.

His meditation was interrupted by a loud noise coming from the side of the small iron gate to his courtyard. It was Nyakoye knocking on the door. The door was opened by Jo. After the usual greetings, they sat down on the front veranda of the house. They are neighbors. Nyakoye had learned from Mr. Faustin that Jo had not gone out this morning. Before leaving for his school, the lycée sainte Marie, where he teaches history, he wanted to spend some time with him.

Tomorrow we will celebrate the AU," says Jo.

Ah, yes!" confirms Nyakoye.

They were not born when the Organization for African Unity was established in 1963 in the Ethiopian capital, Addis Ababa. Jo asked his brother Nyakoye to tell him about this organization that he was pondering.

With a reassuring air, he taught that the OAU was born in circumstances of independence struggle against colonialism, neo-colonialism and foreign imperialism. Historical scourges of serious magnitude that could not be overcome by a single African country. That's why it was necessary to unite to lead this struggle together. He added that the ambitions at the creation of the OAU were numerous, namely :

- To free oneself from the colonial yoke.

- Achieving African Unity.

- Promote development.

- Establish your African identity.

- To be master at home.

- Overcome tribalism, ethnocentrism.

- To bring Africa to play its role in the conduct of world affairs and to contribute to global progress.

To achieve this, he pointed out, several trends were jostling for position and one could note:

- those who advocated African federalism, the creation of a United States of Africa.

- those who advocated for a governmental organization or coordination, a kind of cooperation between states for the realization of integration projects.

- those who were thinking of creating regional groupings, the creation of five regional federations (North, South, East, West and Central).

- those who believed that on a continental level, a confederation of regional federations would be more appropriate than a continental confederation of states.

He concluded that some wanted a political and organic unity, while others wanted a union made of technical and functional cooperation.

On the time frame, there were those who proposed immediate creation and those who foresaw necessary steps.

During his talk, Jo was alerted by Nyakoye's wink on his watch, as if to tell him that he had to leave for school soon in order not to miss his class. Jo, satisfied with his unexpected visit and his enriching explanations, thanked him and they agreed to talk about it soon.

These kinds of contradictory debates and reasoning that bring together fruitful oppositions in order to achieve unity, interest jo.

He knows that dualism in its positive aspect is complementarity. With the third term, which is the reconciler of necessary and fruitful oppositions, the union is realized. This makes him think of relativism, of the law of alternations, of opposites, of the middle way, of the balance by a median way which reconciles the binary. He wondered what would be the conciliating element in the debates succinctly exposed by Nyakoye, the historian? He postponed the answer to his question until later. However, he proposed to first try to understand what had been achieved by the Fathers of Independence. But wouldn't it be better to debate it with others in order to promote a collective awareness? Isn't the debate an efficient way, within the reach of students, of the youth, to commit to the cause of the African Union? Shouldn't it allow for the dream to be dreamt by many?

II. MOBILIZATION TO BRING THE DREAM TO MANY

That day, May 25, was the anniversary of the OAU, which was declared a holiday in his country. Very early in the morning, at 5:20 am, Jo woke up to the favorite melody of his i phone. As usual, he jumped out of bed, put on his clothes and shoes, ran to the door, opened it and ran into the sports field, into his yard. There was a good freshness drenched with scents generously distilled by nature: the blooming of the trees and flowers in the yard and the very characteristic smell of wet earth. It had rained during the night, but Jo didn't know, so much so that his sleep was deep and sweet. It passed pleasantly the gymnastics cadenced by the harmonious songs of morning birds. After forty-five minutes of physical exercise (jogging and muscle stretching), he went to the bathroom and left for GLC University. He had issued invitations to students of all majors to come and participate in the AU debate. A lecture hall was set up for this purpose.

During his breakfast at the kiosk on the university campus, he saw the students come in numbers. Among them were friends and classmates, some of whom shouted his name with joy from afar. Suddenly, he left his table to throw himself into their arms. It was a warm reunion after so many years of separation and forgetfulness. Soon the booth was filled with students who wanted to start the day with cups of tea and latte.

At 8:00 am, without the sound of a bell, they followed each other to go together to the amphitheatre, because usually at this hour, one is already in class or at the work places. Afterwards, Jo started with the prayer of thanks and imploration to God. He also thanked the students who had come in large numbers from different public and private universities. He let them know that the youth is the future of Africa. He explained that as students, they are obliged to play their role and that they are a nursery that will ensure progress and achieve the unity of Africa. But, it is necessary the sacrifice, without which the development would be impossible and there would be nothing good. This morning, he said, we met in this room to exchange on the achievements and the state of progress of the AU, on the one hand, to draw up an overall assessment after the fiftieth anniversaries of independence of our African countries, on the other hand, and finally, to say how we will proceed to achieve the African Union.

Unanimously, Jo was appointed chairman of the meeting and Zebulu was put in charge of the secretariat.

On the first point, Pépé intervened to maintain that the African leaders had indeed succeeded in freeing Africa from the colonial yoke. All African countries have gained their independence. There is no longer a single country that is under foreign tutelage or domination.

Marie, Mamadou, Yalikhatou and others added that this recovery of the sovereignty of the colonized peoples was also supported by the Soviet Union, China and later by some colonizing powers.

Patrice and Kadiatou admitted that the Fathers of Independence also achieved sub-regional and regional integrations that allowed the resolution of many conflicts and that favored the free movement of people and goods, as well as cooperation on the security level and others.

Roland and Hawa pointed out that each country is trying to meet the demands of development and progress on its own and that in reality, the OAU has not yet succeeded in achieving African unity. They wondered then, why the current use of the terms AU instead of OAU. Is this an admission of renunciation or rather an increased and irreversible determination to achieve the ideal?

Following them, Jo declared that "criticism is easy, but art is difficult". He asked that after the fifty years of independence of our States, what have we done, young people, and what is the state of affairs?

On this point, Yaya affirmed that the period beyond the fiftieth anniversary of independence is characterized above all by the fight for democracy. He noted the marked involvement of African youth who are working to have alternation accepted in our states. Almost everywhere in Africa, young people are mobilizing for the establishment of a true democracy and to fight against dictatorship, as well as to refute any other presidential mandate beyond what the constitutions provide. They accept sacrifices at the cost of their lives.

Lila went on to convince that democracy is a universal value that promotes transparency, freedom, debate, efficiency, responsibility, perfection, progress, integration and union. She concludes that no culture or civilization can claim to be the sole repository of it. However, she says, some peoples have achieved improvement by redressing their cultural values.

Still on the subject of the overall observation, it is noted here and there that

The weakness of productivity: they noted that Africa is still far from winning the challenge of food self-sufficiency. They blamed the archaic nature of the means of production. Agricultural techniques remain traditional and large areas of our lowlands and farmlands are impoverished and infected. The result is poor harvests that are largely insufficient to feed the ever-increasing populations. Enough physical strength is expended for little return. For many years, even millennia, many of our ancestors migrated south and elsewhere, having impoverished the lands of central Africa. Today, the host lands are in danger of suffering the same fate, if we are not careful. Our food lands are in a state of desolation. Worse, the effects of climate change will continue to reduce what little fertility they have. Yet, the agricultural sector is essential for our development.

The weakness of industrialization: they noted that on the whole, the economic weight of Africa is not considerable. Most African states are often content to be suppliers of raw materials and outlets for finished products, both in agriculture and mining. In agriculture, the shortcomings of our food and clothing industries force us to consume imported products with all their health and other risks. On the mining level, our soils are increasingly emptied of their natural resources without much benefit. Our mines and agricultural products are bought at low prices, due to our inability to transform them into finished products at home. The fluctuations are at our expense. Our exported mines are transformed in the industrialized countries and then reimported in the form of agricultural materials, electrical materials, transport materials, sanitary materials, construction materials, armament materials, etc.

Absence of an African common market: they noted that also in Africa, each country is satisfied separately from the others, to solve according to its limited capacities at its borders, the challenges related to the circulation of goods, capital and people, to the communication networks and to hydroelectric and solar energies. We can see the fragmentation of markets coinciding with the size of each state, at a time when Europe is creating its common market, between countries that are nevertheless developed.

Political sectarianism: which characterizes the narrow-mindedness of some politicians, intolerant of the opinions of others. The refusal by some heads of state to redress or improve the forms of democracy that have emerged from their traditions. This has often led to dictatorship, contempt for their populations, individualism, egoism, division, ethnocentrism, tribalism, civil wars, corruption, favoritism, mediocrity and everything that demeans. However, they affirm that politics necessarily poses the problem of the value of political action. In this regard, they agree to revalorize the African cultural heritage in the field of political wisdom which rather directs politics towards the sacred, unity, peace, prosperity of the community, understanding between populations, dialogue, consultation, dignity, justice, firmness, order and authority.

This critical analysis of the situation of African states after fifty years of independence aroused revolt in some people. Jo, attentive and noticing the nervousness in the words and gestures of some of the speakers, took the floor to call on everyone to be more lucid and not to lose hope. In a deep voice, he declared that where things seem complicated, the elite must show the way to salvation. Is it not written, he said, "To whom much is given, much will be demanded, and to whom much is entrusted, more will be demanded." ? He asked everyone to suspend the work to take a break before working on the last item on the agenda, namely: what to do?

Once again, they all met at the kiosk to enjoy tea, coffee, fruit juice, yogurt and sandwiches. During this convivial sharing, Howolo, a name that means hare in the Kpèlè culture, told his comrades this story

Once there was a time of abundance and harmony, favored by the generosity of nature. Everything was good. There was balance in the alternating seasons. The flora was marvelous with its meadows, plains, large trees, shrubs, lianas and food plants that produced abundant and highly nutritious fruits, vegetables and tubers. The land was full of organic and mineral substances to allow regeneration. The rivers, swamps and streams were full of fish, crabs, shrimps and other products. It was an environment for the fauna that had diversified and increased. The time of humans had not yet arrived. At that time, the lion had established himself as the master of everything. He abused everything. He exasperated and lost the measure by killing too many animals that he could not eat. He killed for simple pleasure. In his path, there was only desolation, waste and death. His impulses and reflexes were tipping him into madness. The wildlife was tragically reduced by his habits and this should not continue. One day, all the animals, victims, met to find the ideal solution to their misfortunes. Many of them advocated a war against the lions to exterminate them all. But the hare, speaking, asked everyone to avoid war. He dissuaded the others by explaining that the lions were very numerous on earth and that they had managed to build up their strength over the ages, and that war would be even worse than their present condition. If war breaks out, he says, we will be slaughtered even more, especially the weaker ones, among whom I am. What should we do then? To this question, the ant also intervened to forbid the option of extermination which is a nonsense in his eyes and proposed the choice of the union of all to counter or limit the damage of the lions. In this necessary union to overcome adversity, each one will provide as much as he or she can. Thus, immense possibilities would be offered and all linked together for the same goal. The cries of the birds in the sky, out of reach of the lions, will allow the animals to regroup and stand guard. The larger animals will flank to keep the lion from approaching. This imposing and protective look of the union will scare the lion away. As a result, the lion will settle for the little, just enough to survive.

The animals chose this wisdom option given by the ant and life became possible again for all.

With the advent of homo sapiens who took command, the world in its entirety began its degradation in his hands. The lions learned from him the politics of divide and rule: to create discord and disunity by setting one against the other in order to weaken and profit from it later. Individualism and the culture of differences and indifference were established. With the reappearance of their impulses, the lions decided to sow misunderstanding among the animals to achieve, once again, the satisfaction of their morbid desires, which the intelligence of homo sapiens, sapiens allowed them to know. As during their hunts the alarm calls of the birds constituted a major obstacle that thwarted their camouflages, hiding places and plans of attack, they succeeded in disassociating them from the others. They convinced them that since they had united with the other animals, they no longer ate their fill, whereas before they killed as many animals that rotted on the ground within their reach. To the great beasts that formed the belt of protection, they asked them to disunite themselves from the weak ones that are created to be defeated and that it was crazy to want to sacrifice themselves for nothing. Finally, the union broke up to leave the jungle in the forests and bushes, as well as in the human cities and villages. But, let us remember that the antidote is to return to the original union that makes the strength and generates harmony, balance and peace. This story brought satisfaction and many questions in the minds. It was time to return to the amphitheatre.

At 2 p.m., the work resumed with vigor. Comrades, he said, many steps have been overcome. Should we still prolong the transitional period for the creation of the political and organic unity of Africa? Is it necessary to wait any longer? When? Jo asked himself?

In the meantime, he asserts, our states are becoming more and more fragile in the face of the other vast groups constituted: the European Union, Russia, the United States of America and China. Keeping our micro-states in today's world is a serious risk and it will be too late when we have finished squandering or wasting our resources, without solving the problems of development. Before he finished speaking, the other comrades had already stood up, hands in hands, forming the chain of solidarity and all, with the same voice, clamored for the erection of the African Union without further delay. This symbolic gesture rekindled in their hearts and minds the feeling of solidarity that unites and interdependence that binds beings. They had just understood that everything is linked. Jo asked them to take their seats to draw up together a project for the African Union. This project included the following recommendations:

Creation of large modern universities with scientific and technical research laboratories: they denounced the inadequacy of their instructions in the face of the realities of their world. The inadequacies of the educational systems that do not allow them to be critical and balanced. The inefficiency of the training environments and the accompanying structures to produce more young scientists, great innovators. Yet, Africa needs the critical and methodical effort through which the individual accesses reason and conquers freedom and judgment to better act and create. But this cannot be taken for granted. The heads of state talk about their youth, without really taking care of them, except to use them. Yet they are aware of their present and future responsibilities. But, they should have the necessary means to do well. Hence the need to provide them with modern universities, efficient and adequate educational systems, laboratories and scientific and technical research centers that will enable them to give the best of themselves. Africans must appropriate modern sciences and technologies, because poverty and ignorance are not a favourable environment for creation and development. We need an incubation ground for the emergence of geniuses. These means will allow them to carry out scientific research in the fields of fertilizers, environment, agricultural techniques, genetics, sociology, pedology, anthropology, endemic control, medical, epizootic, phytosanitary, pharmacopoeia, cybernetics, philosophy, linguistics, armament, etc. Undoubtedly, the African microstate does not provide the conditions required for such an implementation. It is therefore imperative to unite now to be stronger, because Ebola and so many other scourges or challenges do not wait.

Economic planning and industrialization on a continental scale: they noted that heavy industry requires large investments and thought that the African Union is best suited and capable of such an achievement. They argued that Africa would gain doubly by transforming most of its raw materials and agricultural products into finished products locally. This would create enormous employment and with the benefits of the modern and specialized universities that would be created, there would be a skilled workforce at all levels. Also, Africa could define, itself, the quality and manufacturing standards of its materials, machines, products and others. The result would be a rapid and assured take-off, a development on a consistent basis. We could also make the great rivers and basins of Africa real economic links between the States of the Union and use them to create large hydroelectric dams, in association with solar energy which are considerable natural assets of Africa. We would create trans-African railways, airways and we would maximize the size of the market, constituting an African common market. But these gigantic works cannot really be realized at the size of a single country. That is why we must unite.

Creation of a development bank and an African common market: they noted the need to set up a common bank to support our development. This would put an end to or at least limit the complaints of our States regarding the requirements related to the loans granted by the World Bank which, more often than not, do not suit our interests or the development policy we are aiming at. This requires the raising of funds, the mobilization of large amounts of capital by the African Union from taxes, legacies, contributions and donations. A law would determine the quality of the taxpayer, the quantum, the period of payment and the structure in charge of the collection. History tells us that Africans were forced to make war efforts. To ask them today for an individual contribution, this time, to feed the bank of their own development would be a salutary and commendable initiative.

On the subject of the African common market, they envisaged for Africa, the abolition, one by one, of the barriers erected between the States, which disadvantage the free circulation of goods, services, capital and people. They wished that throughout the economic zone of the African Union, we could freely sell and buy goods and services, following the same regulations. They affirmed that the maintenance of the micro markets of our current States would be against the current of history and progress.

Promoting Democracy and adopting a common Security and Defense Policy: Democracy is close to her heart. Jo asserts that the promotion of democracy, democratic practices would help Africa to move forward. He hopes that these will serve as a common drinking water for the African Union, because of its virtues of freedom, transparency, good governance and good management. A real cure for dictatorship, authoritarianism, individualism, tribalism, ethnocentrism and religious extremism. It is our incontestable rampart.

On the need for a common security and defense policy, they recommended the adoption of common strategies to fight terrorism, internal conflicts, organized crime, drug and human trafficking, cybercrime, climate change and the establishment of an African army.

Solving the problem of inculturation: Numèni notes with regret that the phenomenon of inculturation is a worrying concern today. For most youth, adults and families, swept away by modernity, are increasingly disinterested in their African traditions. However, he declares, our traditions transmit to us a set of consecrated means that allow us to live and to become aware of who we are. These various means are constituted, among others, by :

- Symbols, such as masks, calabash, colas, colors, numbers, water, tattoo, drum, fireplace, etc., materialize the representation of our abstract ideas and remain signs of recognition.

- Rites that are our symbols put into action. The objects used, the figures represented, the gestures made and the words spoken, during our ceremonies of baptism, circumcision, initiation, marriage, funerals, etc.

- Customary practices to resolve conflicts, to express our compliments by refined forms of politeness, to inform (announcement of engagement, marriage, baptism, death and all other social events).

- Rhythms in which our rites are transmitted and performed and which are at the heart of any event or activity.

- Tales, songs, music, dances, games, festivals, sayings, proverbs and myths that express and reveal our origin, our values or virtues, our feelings, our social ties, our understanding of the world, of the divine and in front of life or death, our relationships with others, with the transcendent and with all visible and invisible beings, etc.

He affirms that when an African turns away from his tradition, in favor of the superfluous behaviors of modernism and the unrestrained search for material wealth by all means, he will no longer have a reference point and a reason to live. Uprooted, he will not be able to educate his children either, who risk becoming dangers for others and for the world.

He believes that our current practices in Christianity and Islam are turning us away from ourselves, without good reason, to the detriment of who we are. For example, the fact of imposing to the converted or baptized, the choice of first names of their co-religionists. This distracts us from some of the cultural richness conveyed by customary names. Similarly, he points out that in his culture, first names can determine rank in births and initiation, as well as the particular role and meaning they contain. They can express or represent ideas, virtues, situations, beings and objects. Their existence and spelling in society give assurance to our cultural beliefs and allow us to recognize ourselves, to make the past and the future always present. For example:

Lila: a woman's name that means Peace.

Tinya or Téan : which means Truth.

Nèma: meaning reason is on his side or the one who is right.

Nahoma : means without name, which has no name. Sign of freedom.

Hèni : woman's name which means Gold. A beautiful woman.

Kwèli : which means Panther.

Kwêliko : kwêli = iron. Kow = core. Means core of iron. What is hard and tough.

Numèni : Nu = Man. Mèni = action / event / thing. Means the one who is in humanism.

Holokoulo : Holo = sun. Koulo = to come out. Who makes the sun come out.

Gbona : which means sour.

Gowohagha : which means old calabash.

Gamê : woman's name which means what is above.

Kwêlikolo : means panther skin, a beautiful woman with a long neck.

Tiya: a woman's name which means bowl, etc. Besides these ordinary names, there are also initiation names that Mr. Numèni, who is an initiate, is careful not to mention here.

He maintains that no one can validly convince, except religious extremism, that these customary names would be incompatible with the Evangelical or Islamic messages. Why should we put aside our customary names, when those which are conveyed in the monotheistic religions are also cultural elements? Don't Judaism, Christianity and Islam come from the same Abrahamic tradition, adapted at the beginning to a specific people and which, afterwards, spread and diversified into other cultural forms? he asked. He concludes on the need to root these prophetic religions in our African traditions which offer immense compatible riches.

He also calls on scientists, linguists, specialists in the humanities, researchers, wise men and men of culture to reflect on the possibility for Africa to have at least one common language. He admits that it is an arduous work, but which raises us, honors us and makes us worthy.

He believes that we must allow ourselves to be penetrated by this word of wisdom: "Become what you are". A call to authenticity that puts us in a situation of searching for the truth. A challenge that plunges us into the search for knowledge about ourselves. Yes, to have the love of the knowledge of Africa, of the traditional wisdom. This requires taking into account all that is good in the cultural heritage, in which we are characterized, among others:

-      By our community, family, welcoming and open spirit. A popular culture in which all participate.

- By the love we have for children and their education by all.

- By the respect we give to all life, to parents, to the elderly and to elders.

For him, the whole of all that precedes makes our African humanism which must be revalorized by opening to the world. To make Africa both from itself and from its dialogue with the other cultures of the world. Thus, our African traditions must be places of awareness and communication to validly orient our scientific and technical progress, as well as to enrich our religious convictions. As a proverb says: "Going far is good. To arrive is better". So let us do it by being who we are. Everyone is called to be himself and to be able to give his grain of salt by his model of humanism. By seeking to know each other better, says Numèni, we will facilitate the rapprochement of our populations in order to achieve together the construction of the African Union. It is better to know each other, to identify ourselves so that all together, with the other civilizations of the world, we can make this world beautiful for all.

It was 4:30 pm, and time flew by. Concentration at work and their love for Africa made them forget the notion of time as they approached dusk.

Jo thanked her classmates for giving it their best shot and asked them what to do with the findings of their work. Should this work be limited to them? Should they be satisfied with their mutual enrichment after the debate that had just ended in the amphitheatre? Should the conclusions of their debate remain in the drawers?

In a meeting, they decided on three measures:

- make a written report of their work.

- To share it through social networks, to other students in Africa.

- Organize a march that would be done on June 5.

Before leaving, jo thanks the Good Lord, implores him that each one returns home safe and sound and that the end of each one is good!

They answered amen!

Then, they greeted each other, before leaving. Jo was the last to board the plane. Because of the traffic jams, he returned home at 8 pm.

What a good day, he exclaimed!

After his bath and the evening meal, he calls the secretary and three others on the phone so that they can meet the next day, at break time at the university, to adopt the written conclusions of their debates and share them on social networks, as it has been said. On his bed, he recites a dozen rosaries before falling asleep.

In the morning, as usual, he woke up to the melody of his i phone. The depth of his sleep had left no room for dreams. That day, he decided not to do sports. The urge came to him to go to the morning Eucharistic mass. As a child he regularly attended morning Masses. He was a mass server. After the Eucharistic celebration, he went directly to school. All the trips were made on foot. This habit from his youth, interrupted long ago, came to mind. Suddenly, this desire resurfaced from the depths of his being. Ah, childhood! It conditions our present and future life. Our past that we believe to leave behind us, pursues us everywhere in our states of consciousness and sleep. In his innermost being, he knows that his thirst for God is for all time and it will only be truly quenched when he is called by Him to drink from his source of immortal water. But it is necessary to give ourselves to Him to do His will, knowing that it is by His grace that we are accepted into His Love and not by our works or merits.

In college, he had bean loaf for breakfast. Many people don't want to eat very early in the morning when their stomachs are not demanding anything. Others prefer to eat at the workplace to avoid the delay due to traffic jams in the long way. At the coffee break, Jo met with her classmates to finish their work. Some students joined them. The report presented by the secretary was improved and adopted. They all got involved to share it through social networks. M'mah, Yalamo and Oscar were designated to carry out the administrative formalities for the authorization of the march. The peaceful march was named "Step Forward for the African Union". Each student is urged to use all useful means (telephone calls, meetings, correspondence, messaging, print media, radio, television, social networks), as far as possible, to inform, challenge, raise awareness and encourage other academics in the four natural regions of the country, so that they adhere and add their steps forward for the African Union. This message was spread in the lecture halls, places of prayer, houses, bars, public meeting places and everywhere in the country. In Conakry, three meeting points, namely: UGANC, ICAO and Espace Sory Kandjà Kouyaté were chosen to start the marches at 7:30 am. These steps forward for the African Union should continue to the People's Palace, where the National Assembly is located.

This palace is built in a sacred place called Gbassikolo, between two large baobabs, two of which stood side by side, in pairs, at the edge of the national road, a few meters from the gates of the main palace courtyard. Because of the construction of this road, one of these two baobabs was unfortunately cut. In addition to this main road, there is a second road towards the southern corniche on the sea side and a third road towards the northern corniche that runs along the railroad tracks. These are the roads that lead to the city of Kaloum, Conakry 1. The first occupants of this city were the Bagas. A people rooted in their ancestral tradition, but open and very welcoming. The giant baobab trees in the above-mentioned area are believed to be inhabited by protective genies. It is said that whoever cut down one of the baobabs in the main entrance of the palace courtyard would be struck by a mysterious death.

Now, the days were numbered. There were only ten days left. Yes, ten days separated them from the planned march. Inevitably, this day will come. But what will become of their desire to march? There is the certainty of the succession of days, of the reality of the passing of time, and the uncertainty of the realization of the ambitious walk. What can guarantee us that what is in the making, set in motion, will be realized? Wouldn't the strength of will be the point of support to reach the realization? A firm and persevering will to overcome what seems to us to be above. Jo is convinced that it is necessary to want and to give oneself the necessary means to match the ambition. That is why he and his classmates decided to use the rest of their time wisely. They continued to work, to consult each other, to raise awareness, to encourage each other and to persevere until the day of the march.

Eight days had already passed. These days absorbed by the infinite never come back. The ninth day was also drawing to a close. On the eve of the march, Jo and some of her comrades met at the university campus to take stock of the situation:

- The request for a march was approved.

- Coordination with other university comrades across the country was on point.

- Awareness campaigns were carried out in sufficient quantity.

This time of reunion took only 40 minutes to allow each one to rest, to regain their strength for the big day of the march. Before leaving, Jo asked his comrades to pray to God.

In the cab that took him home, he wrote this poem and sent it to some friends, recommending that they share it with others. Here is the content:

Tomorrow, our will will be active

Our hands clasped on our signs

The rhythm of our words and gestures

Will determine our strength of impact

Our steps forward for the AU will be rhythmic

Similar to the movement of the beating of our animated hearts

Our active will will be directed towards the expressed objective

Nothing is lost from this energy reserved for this much loved construction

A building in which all Africans, with a common will, cooperate

May this strength of will not be an expression of anger

But rather the one that gives life, that perseveres and hopes

For a prosperous tomorrow.

In the evening, as in the night, this poem was spread everywhere. Everyone was eager to see this day.

At home, very early at 8 pm, Jo went to bed to relax. During his sleep, he got up only once to shower, it was 2 am. Then he hurried back to his bed to enjoy his sweet sleep again, because in three hours he would be on the move. This moment arrived and following the ringing of his i phone, he jumped out of his bed, returned to the yard and engaged in a sport, this time, violent: taekwondo and lifting heavy weights. That day, he intensified his sport to capture as much free testosterone as possible. Mr. Jeff, this kind-hearted man, let him in on this and other secrets to well-being. Sweaty and full of energy, he was happy about it. After washing, he spent some time in meditation and prayer before getting dressed. He wore jeans, a white T-shirt and his shoe. Lunch was already finished. It was cassava prepared with a sauce of onions, chilies and other ingredients roasted with red oil from palm nuts. He had eaten five pieces and when he got up to leave, his sister Natalie came to put a lime and garlic in his pockets, although he himself had taken care to wear his rosary. In their environment, it seems that these foods have protective properties against evil spirits and poisonings. Jo accepted these food gifts that he used to eat. On the other hand, some people rather resort to amulets, tattoos, gourmets or bracelets, talismans and especially rings of all kinds. It is not uncommon to find on small frail fingers several overpowering rings. Rings like Kalybos in the clash of the Titans. But if man would instead direct his wickedness against his wicked behaviors, we would be free of these so-called burdens of protection.

III. THE REALIZATION OF THE DREAM

On the morning of the march, the sky was very cloudy. Heavy rains were coming, but nothing could postpone their long-awaited march. Jo took a cab to UGAN, one of the three points of departure for the march. He arrived there at 7 o'clock. It was already crowded. His comrades, in number, came to shake his hands. Joachim, Saïdou, Kèlètigui, Gobu and Agnès took him aside to tell him that they had set up a committee, without his knowledge, to go and consult and do what was necessary with an old reputed person of the place, capable of aborting the rain. This made him think of his friend George's grandfather. It is said that he had the secret of being able to make it rain. He used to mark out the place where he wanted to make it rain. If the rain was scarce during his period, the villagers would resort to him to make it rain. Also, on the occasion of ceremonies or events, they would go to see him again to prevent it from raining. After their unannounced meeting, a beautiful young girl came to meet him in turn to compliment him. She told him that his poetry was beautiful and that she encouraged him to write more poems. Jo smiled at her to express his satisfaction. Together they joined the group.

At 7:20 am, there were thousands of people at UGANC. At the ICAO and at the Espace Sory Kandjà Kouyaté, the courts could not contain the huge crowds present. Finally, the roads were invaded by them. Jo answered the phone calls of the coordinators who were there and asked them to start the march at 7:30 am, as agreed.

Phew! The rain clouds that covered the sky dissipated and gave way to a giant rainbow, with many colors.

What a beautiful weather!" exclaimed Jo.

The crowd of men and women, with rainbow colors, gathered at the UGANC sang the National Anthem before taking the departure. This Anthem speaks of their ideal:

to preach unity, to meet to build the African Unity. On the road, the police were there to coordinate. There was a good understanding. As the marchers advanced, their number increased. In addition to the students, there were tradesmen, unemployed people, civil servants, high school and college students. In passing, all those who were going to their workplaces, showed their sympathy and encouragement. With them, they believe that the future of Africa lies in the African Union. This day, the sky was very favorable to this march. The heavy rain threatening, aborted. The sea breeze, a cool, gentle wind blowing from the sea to the land, comforted them in their march forward for the AU. Voices were raised in this compact crowd to praise the AU. The following words could be heard and read on the placards:

- Long live the AU!

- Strength in numbers!

- The AU, our salvation against dictatorship, ethnocentrism and mediocrity!

- The AU, our greatness and dignity!

- The AU, a factor of freedom and progress!

- The AU, for a responsible youth!

- The AU, the best way to integral development!

- The maintenance of our micro-states = confirmation of colonial imperialism

- The existence of African micro-states will always favor the intervention and domination of colonizing powers.

- AU, to strengthen the scientific and technical capacity of students!

- The AU, to make Africa competitive!

- The AU, for the Great Love!

- The AU, for the democratization of Africa!

- Down with our micro-states!

- Let's break down our walls of separation!

- Long live African federalism!

- The AU, to better manage our human and natural resources!

- Down with selfishness, corruption and fatalism!

- Plural Africa for a common ideal: the AU! etc.

At 10 o'clock, those who started at the Espace Sory Kandjà Kouyaté and at the ICAO reached the Palais du Peuple. Their great number filled the esplanade of this Palace. Jo was informed by his comrades from the other three regions of the country that they were marching at the same time as them. At 10:30 a.m., the group of Jo who had started at UGANC joined the others at the arrival point. Other crowds of men and women continued to stream into the area. The roads were occupied by this human tide. It was like nothing else in the country. In order to unblock the roads and to avoid taking too much time, Jo went up to the platform prepared for this purpose, accompanied by two comrades and made this speech:

Dear comrades!

Brothers and sisters!

Thank you for your overwhelming response to the call to march forward for the AU.

The strength of our firm and persevering will leads us today to the realization of our resolution to march for the AU.

We wanted it and we just accomplished it.

This behavior of those who militate for African Unity belongs from now on to the history which will challenge the other sons of Africa to climb other rungs of the ladder of unity.

But we can only achieve this with others when we understand that beyond our languages, our skin tones, our cultures and geographical positions, there is in the depths of ourselves the same vital deposit that raises us to the heights, by the straight and luminous way, and around which everything is articulated.

This original deposit diversified in the forms following successive adaptations to give the various cultures that we represent.

Yes, we have Africa in common, our motherland.

We are ONE by our origin and we share the same values and have the same existential concerns: belief in the Creator God, solidarity, mutual aid, hospitality, dignity, tolerance, work, courage, respect for one's word, respect due to life, to fellow human beings and especially to the elders, as well as to the elderly, the quest for truth, happiness, prosperity, peace, love, wisdom, harmony between all that exists (visible and invisible), etc. these are the very things that express our principial unity.

No, nothing justifies the confinement of our weakened micro-states within their national borders resulting from colonization, at a time when other countries, though so-called developed and competing, are choosing the path of union to progress together.

Undoubtedly, the fight for progress and integral development cannot be won by our different countries separately, which are also underdeveloped and inefficient in the face of the serious dangers of this world.

Strength in numbers!

Yes, the future of Africa, of its populations, of its youth, is in the African Union which should be encouraged by the other peoples outside of Africa who are well aware of the universal brotherhood linking all humans, so that our world is beautiful.

May God be with us!

As he came down from the rostrum, his comrades, happy, raised their arms and declared loudly: Let the debates continue! Let's not cross our arms! After warm greetings and reciprocal thanks, everyone returned to their homes in joy.

Jo took a cab to her home. In the capital of his country, cabs are commonly used for travel. The buses, which are mainly used by pupils, students and civil servants, are not numerous in the traffic, because when they break down, they deteriorate and rot during the long time they are parked, due to the lack of spare parts on the national market. A badly organized business. During the trip in the cab, we heard on the different radio stations, comments on the marches for the AU carried out in the whole country. Jo listened attentively. In N'zérékoré, one of the four regions of the country, a program broadcast the reactions of the marchers who denounced, among other things

- The harmful behavior of certain political leaders who do not want unity and who use all diabolical means to sow discord, division and war between the once peaceful Kpèlè and Koniaké populations.

- The fact that a village in this forest region, named Zowota, was invaded at night by highly militarized and intentionally deployed convoys to kill and shoot at point-blank range villagers caught sleeping, under the pretext that people in this village were opposed to the activities of a mining company. There has been no investigation and no justice to date. This criminal and villainous behavior comes from an army that is believed to have been reformed.

- Also because of a criminal act provoked, concerning some individuals of another village, in the same region, called Nwomêi, strongly armed soldiers were again deployed there to besiege this village. It was recommended that the village be razed to the ground, which caused the villagers to flee, one of whom, while pregnant, gave birth in the bush in their desolate peregrinations. The village was emptied of its inhabitants and all their belongings were looted by the new armed occupants, and other exactions that are only practiced in small countries locked in dictatorship and underdevelopment, against which the African Union constitutes a bulwark.

- Finally, they recalled in bitterness that well before the reform, the same Guinean army presented to the world, on September 28, 2009, its tragic scenes of rape and massacres, how horrifying, on our sisters and brothers gathered at the September 28 stadium to participate in a political meeting.

Jo entered the house at 4:30 pm. After his bath, he went to the table, so much that he wanted to eat. Usually, he only eats when he is hungry. While resting on his bed, he fell asleep quickly, because of the fatigue. At 11 p.m. he woke up after six hours of uninterrupted, deep and very restful sleep. There were people in the living room who were still watching TV. Not wanting to get up, he let himself be carried away by the meditation on certain ancient mysteries of the world which were told to him, in particular on the mysterious powers to make the rain fall and to prevent it from raining, to transform himself into a snake, a buffalo, a lion, a panther, a cat, an agouti, a warthog, a crow, an owl, a bat, a bee, a tree, a fish...to avoid death by taking the life of others, by exchanging oneself, to predict the future by the game of cowrie shells, of sands or by simple sight, to have invisible beings at one's service, to have someone beguiled, even if he is far away and to cast spells on him by gestures and incantations, to eat things without being in visible contact with them, to be invincible in fights, to achieve superhuman feats thanks to magic, to walk on water, to live under water, to make long journeys, in an invisible form, therefore without being seen, in a period of time, to make oneself invisible, to see and converge with the dead, to use the parts or elements of a deceased person for magical purposes and so many things still unknown to men about life, the eye that sees beyond the ordinary eyes, prophecies, destiny and incomprehensible situations that happen to us...

He remembered the story of his friend Paul who told him that one day he went to his village to spend his vacations with his grandfather. This one belongs to the family of the first occupants. In this village, there is also the family of those who perform the village sacrifices, because of their sacrificial offering, on which the village tree was planted, following a particular rite. There is also the family of the warriors, of those who protect the village and many other families with specific roles. In their village, there are rivers, swamps and streams. One morning, his grandfather took him to his hamlets where his crop fields are located near a river. When they reached the liana bridge over the river, which served as a passage, he took him around to the forest side. There, he made him cross over the water, on something like a tree trunk placed slightly under the water, without a visible support, while the bottom is very deep and the passage so long, that a wood could not have such a length. The old man recommended that he simply put his feet on the spot where he passed. After visiting the hamlets filled with food: rice, taro, yams, corn, beans, cassava, potatoes and peanuts, he left the old man sitting in a hut without telling him where he was going. It was to go and see the curious bridge over which his old man had made him pass. Against all expectations, he went to find his grandfather on the spot, whom he left behind. The latter told him that if he had come to check the bridge they had used as a passage, he would not see it, because the floods would have swept it away. Jo wondered inwardly how the old man had arrived there, unseen, when Paul had gone off alone, leaving him sitting in the hut, and how he knew that he had come to check, to satisfy his curiosity.

He told her that another day, his old man asked him to accompany him to a nearby village. They got up very early in the morning to leave, because of the distance between the two villages. During the journey, he could not take it anymore, so much so that he was exhausted, while his old man held on. In shame, he sincerely told his old man that he was really tired. The latter smiled at him and used tree branches, by which he whipped his feet, then those of his grandson and suddenly, they saw each other on the outskirts of the village. Paul was greatly surprised and amazed. On the way back from the village, his grandmother informed him that his grandfather wanted to empty himself into him, passing on his mystical secrets and soon he would be brought in to be initiated. Frightened, he quickly left the village to join his parents in the capital.

He also told her that in the area of her village there is a river that is feared because of its death traps against humans. There are frightening, deep and mysterious places where the water of the river is always cloudy and blackened. It is enough to lean close to it or to plunge lightly the foot or the hand in these places of the river to see oneself precipitated in the depths, as if something drew irresistibly downwards, in the entrails of the mortal abyss.

He also told him that in another village, two hunters went hunting one day at night. One asked the other to be ready at a place he indicated. He told him his hunting plan, which consisted in going to get some game to lead them into the trap, in order to allow his friend who was already posted, to be able to shoot at point blank range at the game that would pass through in a chain. But, he took care to inform the other, that he would transform himself into an animal and that on the way back to the trap, he would be at the head of the line and that he should not shoot at the first game that would cross. Against all odds, as the group of animals advanced, the hunter, well posted, shot at the first animal to cross and curiously his friend was killed. The paradox is that one shoots at an animal and it is a man who dies as a result of the wound on this animal. Can man have several bodies? Can the same spirit live successively in several different bodies?

Moreover, he informed him that those who transform themselves into agoutis at night, to go and devastate the rice fields of others, often go in groups so that if one of them is trapped, the others come to rescue him from the clutches of death. Is it not mysterious to see a man momentarily abandon his body to live in the body of an animal and to see that everything that happens to this animal is reflected in the human body? How can we understand and explain this other mystery of incarnation?

Jo again remembered what he was told about a lawsuit against a villager. This man was accused of grazing a rice field at night in his animal form, that is, by transforming himself into an agouti. On his way to court to answer his summons, he carried a few feet of rice in his bag. During his defense, he showed the judge the rice plans and declared that the accusation against him could not validly stand, because a human, he said, as far as he knew, could not graze, eat and digest these straws and rice stems, unfit for his consumption. In case of dispute, he asked to be shown the contrary proof, by swallowing these few straws and stalks of rice taken away. This was the end of the trial in his favor, because he had no one to do it. One might as well say that this mystical universe is the opposite of science. It is impenetrable by scientific methods. Yet the accused man has this devastating power. The others with whom they share this secret know that he is the culprit, but unfortunately the court dismissed him from the case for an unproven crime.

It was also told that during a game of supremacy, the sorcerers sowed grains of rice on the ground. Thanks to their magical powers, they would have made them germinate, grow until the flowering and maturation of the grains, which would be harvested and crushed to make the seeds available for preparation, in the same day, during the time of the game.

In pharmacopoeia, there are traditional healers who claim to be helped or guided by invisible spirits: genies or the dead. Hundreds of medicinal plants and medical products are known in the absence of scientific analysis. By embracing science, modern research and pharmaceutical manufacturing laboratories can enhance this very promising sector.

Jo's meditation led him to the crossroads: of the ambiguity of life, of the incomprehensibility of man, of the complexity of things, of other ways and laws at the antipodes of science and natural laws, of uncertainty and doubt. His reflection on mystical traditions led him to question the nature and value of these traditions. But how could he know it or know it when he is outside of them? He knows that to access mystical knowledge, one must first be initiated. He could go there, but he is afraid of losing his freedom afterwards. Because there, it seems, one commits himself to keep absolute silence on the ordeals he will have undergone, on all that he could hear and discover, as well as on all that he will see and know, under penalty of a horrible and mystical death. Once one becomes a man under oath, one is condemned never to reveal any of the secrets to anyone who is not qualified to know them, nor to write them down, nor to reproduce them in any other way. However, he believes that it is time to reflect deeply on the traditions, to rectify them and to bring them into line with today's life, in order to achieve integral development, progress, harmony and beauty in the work of human construction and the world. But is this attitude of searching for the truth in freedom possible in the deep village, where curiosity, questioning, debate, criticism, change and doubt are little appreciated, even forbidden, like the forbidden fruit in the lost paradise. Therefore, the risk of seeing his wings burned in his quest for light, in the conditions mentioned above, leads him to give up.

After an hour of meditation, he fell asleep again and only woke up when his alarm clock rang in the morning.

The day after the march, the universities were abuzz with activity. It was time for reports, comments, congratulations and thanks. Happy and hopeful students expressed their joy. In several African countries, their march was in the headlines and left room for debate.

Days passed without resemblance. In Bamako, Republic of Mali, and Acra, Republic of Ghana, pro-AU civil societies also decided to demonstrate. Marches, major debates and cultural evenings took place in these and many other countries that followed suit for the AU. There was emulation and sharing of ideas. The general agreement of academics in all regions of Africa led to a continental meeting of their leaders in Conakry, scheduled for December 25, seven months after the founding of the AU.

after the AU party, to address some of the concerns expressed about the Union.

Jo and his comrades, honored and amazed by this news, set up an organization allowing students from other African countries to be lodged and taken care of free of charge during their stay by the students' families in Conakry, the place of the meeting. This approach highlighted the African hospitality and favored the reciprocal knowledge of Africans among themselves.

On the day of the meeting at the GLC university campus, Jo proposed that the chairmanship and secretariat be provided by a Ghanaian and an Ethiopian. Three items were on the agenda: - the framework of the union, - the form of the union - and miscellaneous.

On the framework of the union, the students approved everything that had been admitted by their fathers, namely: a union encompassing the continental African states, Madagascar and the islands bordering Africa. On the other hand, Jo advocated a softening, an opening to any independent state claiming to be from Africa and which would accept the principles of the latter. Thus, geographical proximity would not be the only determining element of the framework of the African Union.

On the form of the union, the debate was abundant. But finally, the ideas converged on African federalism: the Community of African States. They noted that the union is only possible between those who exist. Nowadays, in the African space, there are only political entities in the form of States. There is no regional grouping or regional federalism yet. So, if it is decided today to create a union, it will be done by the existing states. This does not exclude the possibility of a grouping by those states that want to form a single political entity that would promote the integration of large groups acquired for this African federalism. They agreed that this union would be based on three Powers: - Federal Executive Power, - Legislative Power and the Judicial Power. But to define the relations between them and their functioning, as well as for the creation of other mechanisms, institutions and organs for a good organization and administration, they strongly recommended the assistance and the expertise of other African sons more qualified, more cultivated, more intelligent and wiser, in order to make us avoid the pure and simple mimicry which would not correspond to our African identity.

On the last point, they demanded that a one-page letter be sent to the President of the African Union, expressing the concern of the African students, which would be sent to all African Heads of State. The letter was written and sent the next day, so that the guests could travel the following day.

It was written:

To His Excellency, the President of the African Union.

Excellence,

We, the African students, have the honor to express to you our joy to see you assume the noble duties of the presidency of the African Union and to encourage you in your tireless efforts of reform to achieve Unity.

We are aware that steps have already been taken to reach this level. We remain grateful to our forefathers and elders in this construction site of the African Union.

However, the serious dangers of this world, the demands of integral development, the fragility of our micro-states and our African values, incite us to courageously climb other rungs of the ladder of unity to achieve federalism of our African states which will be our strength and our pride.

We African students are more and more reassured that in order to be competitive, useful to ourselves and to others, it is imperative to put at our disposal adequate educational systems, modern universities with scientific and technical research laboratories that a single African state could not afford.

Yes, the future of Africa is in African Federalism, which must not be delayed.

That is why we urge you to discuss it in council with the other Heads of State, open to former African Heads of State.

In the meantime, please accept, Excellency, the expression of our deepest respect.

On December 26 in Sékhoutouréyah, the delegation of African students was received by the President of the African Union. After fruitful exchanges and the transmission of the correspondence previously read, he addressed his encouragements to them and committed himself to take charge of the travel expenses of the students coming from the other States. They were satisfied and thanked him for his availability and generosity. The students' voluntary contributions and the financial assistance of some of their parents made it possible to ensure the travel of their guests in the city and to organize that day a dance for them.

At 7:00 pm, they ate together a meal composed of several dishes well furnished, where each one found his tastes and preferences. On the dining tables prepared for this purpose, there were dishes of salads, rice, couscous, fonios, to, foutu made of yam, banana, corn, akèkè, spaghetti, potato and bean fries, accompanied by fish, chicken and beef. In the fruit baskets, there were oranges, limes, pineapples, bananas, papayas, avocados, grapefruits, mangoes, watermelons and apples. There were also soft and alcoholic drinks, as well as cow's milk contained in calabashes. The service was free and everyone ate to their hearts content. During the meal, the guests who had gone for a walk by the sea told how beautiful it was to be there to enjoy the benefits of nature:

- From the immensity of the ocean, from this salty sea water, stretched as far as the eye can see, from its rising and undulating waves making innumerable small balls of water appear, whose floats and fallout produce white flies, bringing fresh and soft wind. A rising tide that drains all the dirt (plastics, packaging, objects, household waste, clothing and others) from people to the shores. It is the return to the sender. This natural cleaning by the sea could encourage humans to be environmentally or ecologically responsible.

-       From nightfall, when the sun in the west, glowing, offered a dazzling spectacle with its great ball of faint rays that reflected on the sea multiple fantastic colors.

-       Of these birds in parade which dived and dived again in this mass of water to bathe and to feed.

-       Of those sweaty people who, after their sports, threw themselves into this salt water to benefit from its therapeutic virtues.

Amazed, they wanted to stay longer, but it was almost time for the festive dinner. They had to leave to eat together with the others, because there is a time for everything. However, they questioned the validity of the constructions made in the sea and its surroundings, which deprived the population of free access and reduced the development spaces for all. They asked their comrades to denounce and oppose this policy of anarchic and selfish urbanization, while this beautiful and beneficial sea was offered freely by the Creator of the world for all, without exclusion. It is therefore up to humans to better manage this natural resource, threatened moreover by climate change whose harmful effects will cause the waters to rise.

The sharing of this evening meal, taken together, gave rise to fruitful exchanges, to moments of joy, laughter and pleasure that continued into the dance hall.

The animation of this dance party was entrusted to a very experienced specialist, named Jean-Baptiste, who knew how to satisfy the sensibility of each one thanks to his numerous carefully selected musical varieties. The guests were the most requested by the girls. Here, the stranger is welcome and best pampered. The students who were deprived of their girlfriends from time to time said with a laugh: do you see how far hospitality goes? In any case, everything was done to make the guests feel comfortable. It was an unforgettable moment. The enjoyment ended late in the night. The guests were escorted back to their host homes to allow them to rest a little before they left during the day. Jo made sure that everything went smoothly.

During the day of the 27th, the hosts, happy with their warm welcome, addressed their sincere thanks to the families of accommodation, to their comrades and to the Guinean people, before taking the roads of the return, by promising never to cross the arms.

The Chairman of the African Union, in his wisdom, expedited the response to the students' request, by consulting the other African and Madagascar Heads of State. By mutual agreement, they decided to put it on the agenda of their next meeting.

Students and civil societies across Africa continued to mobilize for the cause of African Union. Increasingly, the movement took on a continental scope, as if the people were thirsty for this longed-for unity. Hadn't the oracles predicted a continental revolution in Africa without bloodshed? It is better, because too much human blood has already stained the earth. May God forgive us!" exclaimed jo.

From day to day, from night to night, everyone's attention was focused on the African Heads of State Summit. This summit conference took place. On the eve, prayers were said in churches, mosques, sacred forests and other places of worship. When the day came, the world was curious to know the conclusions of the Heads of State gathered. What will be decided? Will there be dissension? Will the African Union be accepted by all? Some people were anxious and stressed, while others were serene. Jo was among the calm and serene. He thought that the invitation made to the former African Heads of State and to some Great Men, such as Mr. François Hollande, Barak Obama and others to this summit augured a good thing, a success.

In offices, workshops, fields, in the bush, on the sea, in markets, in cars, in houses, on the roads, everywhere, people were tuned in to the different radio and television stations that relayed information about the summit. It was said that at 6:30 pm, the

President of the African Union would report on the Africa 24 channel. Nobody wanted to miss this historic and sublime moment. A few of Jo's comrades met at his home to follow the events together. It was almost time. Any moment now the conclusions of the summit will be announced.

Ah, today is the future! exclaimed Zebulus.

At Africa 24, the President of the African Union stepped forward with elegance and a smile. The moment seemed interrupted, as if time did not exist. The president's every gesture was scrutinized, interpreted to know what would be said. Fortunately, his smile was a strong signal that calmed hearts. Without hesitation, he proclaimed the good news:

African people!

Beloved brothers and sisters!

The Union will be sealed between all our African States. The Heads of State gathered at the summit have unanimously chosen the Union of our States in a federal framework.

Within three months, each country must hold a referendum so that each of you can express yourselves freely on this choice of the Union.

At the end of this period, we will meet again to work on the constitution and other issues.

That is why, until then, we call upon the African intelligentsia: our scholars, men of culture, sages, professors, academics, researchers and all other capacities, to get in touch with the secretariat of the Union, in order to organize a common work, so that all that will be adopted expresses our identity values.

Let's love each other!

Thus ended this good news on a note of LOVE.

Applause erupted from everywhere with shouts of joy. Tears in the eyes. Very quickly, jubilant crowds took over public places and roads to sing and dance. The sounds of tamtam, flutes, whistles, balafons and other musical instruments echoed through the city. The good atmosphere presaged a vote in favor of the Union referendum. The night would be tumultuous. Jo took care to buy three liters of palm wine, newly harvested with fruit juices, coffee and tea to feast with his comrades at home. While sharing a meal, they exchanged and deciphered the message that was being broadcast.

Jo interpreted this message in these loose verses:

Africans! We are all sisters and brothers

Challenged to love one another

And to unite us by free consent

To build the community of African states

From now on, we will progress together

Holding the hands of the weakest

In the respect of our identity values

Open to the world

After this interpretation approved by the others, they all raised their glasses to show their joy and to wish each other long life and prosperity.

In the message, Zebulus noted the necessary link between norms and identity values. She argued that the rule of law must indeed be based on our identity values. However, she stated that in the legal field and many others, African intellectuals are often satisfied with the simple reproduction in their national positive laws of the legal norms enacted by their former colonial powers, without worrying about the conformity of these norms to our African cultures. A work of pure and simple mimicry.

However, she asserted that all the imported legal texts do not express our identity values and the legitimate aspirations of our African populations.

It gave the example of the repressive system which is based essentially on the application of prison sentences. Misdemeanors and most crimes are punished by imprisonment, which consists in holding convicted offenders in a closed house, depriving them of their freedom. They are immobilized there, crammed without being able to do anything. They withdraw into themselves, in laziness, idleness, until the end of the sentence. In the meantime, they are fed and cared for by the state, as far as possible, without any contribution from them. They are maintained in the irresponsibility that is antinomic, the opposite of the awareness, of the amendment. She pointed out that most of the houses of incarceration constitute nests of big banditry, where inhuman behaviors are inherited.

In African wisdom, work is glorified. Everyone must work. She affirmed that in the past, in the villages, one could not find a single able-bodied person during the day, because they all went out very early in the morning for field work and other tasks and returned at dusk.

It concludes that since work ennobles man, it is therefore better to make more use of forced labor for public interest, for the sanitation, cleaning and maintenance of roads, drainage channels, public places, road construction, railways, development of large lowlands, plains, agricultural activities, livestock, reforestation and others, so that they manage to feed, during the time of detention, the fruits of their work.

She added that the establishment of an adequate monitoring system, an intelligent and efficient organization, as well as the prior realization of certain logistical and other conditions will make it possible to achieve this ideal.

A few sips revived their hearts more and more. Zebulus asked Jo what his explanation or speech might be for the last words of the message: "Let us love one another. Jo smiled, then laughed. He declared that he can only sing about love.

Before he had finished saying the last word, his guests, in a rush, gently asked him to sing this love. Closing his eyes for a little while of contemplation, he opened his eyelids to sing in these words:

The movements of our hearts carry us towards you, Africa

And with respect to your embodied values

And to your sons: sisters and brothers

All together determined to build the African Union

Our love is the benevolence that wants the good of the other

Not a love of concupiscence

Who simply wants to take over from the other

With an immoral purpose

For it is a love that has been forged over the ages

Crystallized by progressive fixation

True love

Dispute of the ephemeral love at first sight

A love based on free renunciation

From the only individual good

To counteract selfishness

In order to activate our African solidarity

The intensity of this love carried

Gives the state of the light

Who will guide us in the quest for truth

Which reveals to us that love is life

A life that is a gift

But a gift that is given back

In an unbroken chain

This is the principle.

This song of jo plunged his guests into a dream. Each one found its account there and interpreted it freely according to its capacities. An inexhaustible poetry in the image of the sung love.

One of the guests did not hesitate to call jo a dreamer. It is certain that the birds of ill omen are often the closest to us. As it was getting late, his guests asked to leave. They say good things don't last long. Jo didn't need to fetch his torch to see them off. That day, the countless stars in the sky were watching over the earth with their illuminating lights. On the way back, one could see here and there, gatherings of people celebrating. It was a good opportunity for a solitary or couple walk. The evening humidity and the fresh wind created a more or less cold atmosphere. There was music everywhere. Folk songs and dances, as well as modern music animated the city. Cabs were still running. So easily, Jo found one. After shaking hands, his comrades embarked, except for Zébulu who made a very pleasant surprise, by agreeing to stay with Jo to spend the night together. Amazed by this unforgettable surprise, this one strongly tightened it in his broad well muscled chest. It was the departure of their friendship. This hidden desire in Jo's heart was discovered by Zebulu's sixth sense which allowed their shared love to blossom.

Upon his return to the country, the Guinean President organized the first referendum vote, which took place on a Sunday, a blessed day. Contrary to the usual votes that took place in tension, cheating, demagogy, pressure and nervousness, this vote was well received by all. It was an occasion for a national celebration enriched by the specificities of the four natural regions of the country. In the forest region, in N'zérékoré, the masks for the celebrations of the festive events came out to make the party more beautiful.

On the great occasions of festivities, the masks come out in pairs: a mask with a male figure next to the mask with a female figure to entertain. This results from the playful function of the masks. Here, the ritual is very light. These masks are a wooden sculpture worn on the face with a special costume that hides the whole body. Its accoutrements are made of raffia, clothes, animal skins, cowrie shells, animal hair and others with specific colors for each male and female mask. There were also masks on stilts. These masks walk on a long stick made of bamboo or other prepared wood, to walk at a certain height above the ground. They too are completely covered by their special costumes. Animal horn trumpets, drums and lutes: large, medium and small djembes, bells, armpit drums, djabaras, bells, braided rattles, dance bracelets, dance belts and other folk music instruments chanted the steps of dances and songs of the land. This referendum did not record any no votes or opposition to African federalism. There were no unfortunate or untoward incidents. Isn't the African person naturally inclined towards solidarity and community? Is this referendum test not a demonstration?

Then followed the yeses of the other African populations of Algeria, Angola, Benin, Botswana, Burkina Faso, Burundi, Cameroon, Cape Verde, Central African Republic, Comoros, Republic of Congo, Democratic Republic of Congo, Ivory Coast, Djibouti, Egypt, Eritrea, Ethiopia, Gabon, Gambia, Ghana, Guinea Bissau, Equatorial Guinea, Kenya, Lesotho, Liberia, Libya, Madagascar, Malawi, Mali, Morocco, Mauritania, Mauritius, Madagascar, Malawi, Mauritania, Niger, Nigeria, Senegal, Senegal, Uganda, and Uganda, Guinea Bissau, Equatorial Guinea, Kenya, Lesotho, Liberia, Libya, Madagascar, Malawi, Mali, Mauritius, Mauritania, Morocco, Mozambique, Namibia, Niger, Nigeria Rwanda, Sao Tome and Principe, Senegal, Seychelles, Sierra Leone, Somalia, Sudan, South Sudan, Swaziland, Tanzania, Togo, Tunisia, Uganda, Zambia and Zimbabwe.

Jo, amazed, wrote this poem for Africa:

Tree of Africa

Oh! Great tree of Africa!

You my Africa

That I exhort and invoke

You make our unity

Nourished by the same sap

Drawn from your rectified values

Coming from your entrails

We make up your unrivalled branches

But all fixed on your unique marbled trunk

Without lament, but in love and unity

So that together we can give you back your strength and your beauty

In your thick and multicolored foliage

Will shelter innumerable beings

Who will come from all the horizons of the earth

To make it their refuge

The smell of your bloom will be attractive

Your fruits will give life and knowledge

So that you stand solidly in the middle of the storms

And unshakeable until the eschatological day

By your vertical stature, turned towards the starry sky

You will remain grateful to the beloved Creator

Who gave you everything

So that in return, you give.

Mr. Joseph Kolèmou, lawyer, was born on 24/02/1968 in Kissidougou. He did his primary and secondary studies in N'zérékoré and high school in Samoé. After the philosophical cycle at Saint Augustin de Bamako, he returned to Guinea where he obtained a Master's degree in Law in 1995 and the CAPA in 1998. He is an individual lawyer.

> **The greatness of a united Africa will be achieved through the union of its micro-states whose borders are the result of colonization. But beyond this great continental space, the true greatness lies in the values or virtues that the African people embody. The exploration with discernment and rectification of African traditions, leads to the rapprochement of all its populations in an African Union. And faced with the great challenges of development, progress and the enormous dangers of this world, it is now necessary to rely on the political and organic unity ensured by the federation of its states: the Community of African States to be built. This African Unity, which must be encouraged by other peoples outside the African continent, will allow Africa to better participate in the conduct of the affairs of this world, to contribute to global progress, to defend its identity by bringing its grain of salt, by its model of humanism, so that all together, with other civilizations of the world, we can make this world beautiful. To achieve this, young scholars and elites in various activities must play a leading role.**

yes
I want morebooks!

Buy your books fast and straightforward online - at one of world's fastest growing online book stores! Environmentally sound due to Print-on-Demand technologies.

Buy your books online at
www.morebooks.shop

Kaufen Sie Ihre Bücher schnell und unkompliziert online – auf einer der am schnellsten wachsenden Buchhandelsplattformen weltweit! Dank Print-On-Demand umwelt- und ressourcenschonend produzi ert.

Bücher schneller online kaufen
www.morebooks.shop

Printed by Books on Demand GmbH, Norderstedt / Germany